Reptiles of North America

Billy Grinslott & Kinsey Marie Books

ISBN - 9781965098516

Musk turtles. This species rarely emerges to bask in the sun and is most likely seen in darker conditions. Musk turtles climb really-well and can be seen resting in trees. They got their name, because they have glands around the edges of their shells that release a chemical with an unpleasant odor, like musk, to deter predators. An odor so vile, it has earned this turtle the nickname stinkpot. Musk turtles walk on the bottom of ponds and streams instead of swimming. Musk turtles can live to be 40 to 60 years old.

There are many types of softshell turtles around the world. Unlike most other turtles, their shell is soft, flat, and rubbery. These turtles are also able to breathe underwater, unlike many other turtles. When the softshell turtle is scared, it will burry itself in the sand, with only it's head sticking out. The Spiny softshell turtle is one of the largest freshwater turtle species in North America.

The red-bellied Cooter is a turtle with a dark shell and a distinctive red belly. Red-bellied Cooter's are also called the redbelly turtle. They are usually found in areas with deep, fast-moving water. The red-bellied Cooter is the largest recorded basking turtle. These turtles are extremely shy and easily scared. They live in areas with lots of aquatic vegetation, a muddy bottom, and deep, fast-moving water. They bask on logs, rocks, woody debris, and manmade rafts to regulate their body temperature.

The bog turtle is one of the smallest living turtles. You may think you've found a baby turtle, but adult bog turtles only grow up to about 4 inches long. America's smallest turtle is the bog turtle. Bog turtles are very rare, less than 10,000 are estimated to be left in the wild. Bog turtles live in the eastern United States. Bog turtles can live over 60 years in the wild.

Spotted Turtles got their name because of the colored spots on their shell. Interestingly, this species will only eat when they are under water. No two spotted turtles ever have the same pattern of spots. Spotted turtles are one of the smallest turtle species in the US.

The painted turtle is one of the most common turtle species in North America. Painted turtles must be in the water while they eat. Their tongues do not move freely, so they need to be underwater to swallow. A turtle's shell is made up of about 60 bones. To help them move efficiently through the water, Painted Turtles have flat shells and webbed feet. Painted turtles can grow to be 4 to 7 inches long. Painted turtles are diurnal, meaning they are most active during the day. They spend most of their day basking in the sun. Painted turtles eat vegetation, insects, snails, small crayfish, and fish.

The spiny softshell turtle has spines on the front of its shell. Spiny softshell turtles can breathe underwater using their snorkel-like snout. Spiny softshell turtles can hibernate underwater in the winter for months, absorbing oxygen through their mouth and cloaca. Spiny softshell turtles are sometimes called pancake or leatherback turtles because of their unique shell. Spiny softshell turtles are bimodal breathers, meaning they can breathe both in air and underwater. Spiny softshell turtles eat almost anything in the water that will fit into their mouth.

The Wood turtle is a medium-sized turtle native to North America. The wood turtle gets its name from its shell, which resembles engraved wood as it ages. Each year a new scute grows under the old one, but unlike many other turtle species, the old scute's do not fall off. Wood turtles spend much of their day basking in the sun. Wood turtles have a unique hunting method called the worm stomp, where they stomp their feet on the ground to make worms come out of the soil. Wood turtles can live to be over 70 years old.

Map turtles get their name from the lines on their shell that look like a map. Mature females are twice the length and 10 times the mass of mature males. Map turtles are dormant from November through early April, spending most of their time underwater, under submerged logs, or in the mud at the bottom of a lake. Map turtles are diurnal, meaning they are more active during the day and sleep more at night. Most turtles don't have teeth but instead have hardened beaks they use to tear their food.

There are many different types of Box turtles. Box turtles got their name because unlike most turtles, they can completely close-up into their shell, much like a box. They have a hinged belly that can close so tightly that even an ant couldn't get inside. Like a bear, a box turtle will hibernate during winter. Every box turtle has unique markings on their shell and head that help them blend in with the forest floor. Box turtles have a homing instinct that allows them to navigate back to their home base, even if they're in an unfamiliar area. Box turtles have all sorts of fun and quirky behaviors. They like making friends.

Snapping Turtles have one of the strongest jaws of most turtles. They can't retract their head into their shell, like other turtles, so their instinct is to bite things to protect themselves from danger and that's how they got the name snapping turtle. Snapping turtles are essentially nocturnal, as this provides them with the perfect time to feed. Snapping turtles are very fast swimmers.

Snapping turtles can weigh up to 75 pounds. Snapping turtles can live up to 50 years in captivity and 30 years in the wild.

Gopher tortoises are named because of their ability to dig large, deep burrows like gophers. They have specialized shovel-like front legs that help them to dig, and their back legs are strong and sturdy. Some burrows will be 40 feet long. Gopher tortoises can live up to 60 years in the wild. They are considered and endangered species.

The Slender glass lizard looks like a snake, but it's a lizard. Slender glass lizards have moveable eyelids, which distinguishes them from snakes. A slender glass lizard can break off its tail as a defense mechanism when threatened. The tail will continue to move, distracting the predator while the lizard escapes. The tail will regrow back to normal. Slender glass lizards hibernate in areas where its cold. Slender glass lizards are nonvenomous and are not poisonous.

Green anole lizards can change color based on their mood, temperature, and health. They can appear bright green when they are active, and warm, and brown when they are cold or sleeping. Males have a colorful skin flap on their throat called a dewlap that they can extend to attract other anoles or defend their territory. Green anoles live in the southeastern United States.

Italian wall lizards are considered a pest, because they populate rapidly. They can live in many different habitats, including grasslands, meadows, coastal dunes, and urban areas. They are often found on walls, fences, and rocks. They can also adapt to different climates. They will hibernate in cold climates and can supercool themselves in hotter climates. They are shy and extremely fast-moving lizards.

Night lizards are small, ranging from less than 1.6 inches to over 4.7 inches in length. Night lizards can change their color to blend in with their surroundings. Example, they can change from light olive in the evening to dark brown during the day. Night lizards have pupils that open wide in low light conditions, allowing them to see in the dark. Night lizards are good climbers. Night lizards are nocturnal during the hot summer months, that's how they got their name. Night lizards eat spiders, termites, and other insects.

Chuckwallas can be tan, brown, black, yellow, or orange, which helps them to blend into the rocky desert habitat. Chuckwallas are primarily herbivores, eating leaves, flowers, and fruit. Occasionally they will eat insects. Chuckwallas can grow up to nine inches long. They are the second largest lizard in the southwestern United States. When threatened, they will inflate their lungs and wedge themselves into rock crevices, making it hard for predators to remove them.

Long-nosed leopard lizards can change color from a lighter cream to a darker brown or gray. They eat both plants and animals, including insects, smaller lizards, rodents, berries, and leaves. Their body can grow up to six inches long, with their tail being equally as long. These lizards prefer sandy and rocky areas with some vegetation for cover and lots of open space to run. When threatened, they make a hissing sound.

Southern alligator lizards live in coniferous forests, oak woodlands, grasslands, and along creeks. They prefer shelter under rocks, logs, and wooden boards, and in tall grass. Southern alligator lizards sleep almost fully submerged under water, that's how they got their name. Southern alligator lizards can be brown, gray, green, or yellowish, with dark crossbands and white spots. Southern alligator lizards eat mostly insects, spiders, snails, and slugs, but large adults may also eat small lizards and bird eggs. Southern alligator lizards can detach their tail as a defense mechanism, and it will grow back.

Northern alligator lizards can be found in woods, grasslands, and near the bases of buildings. They can grow to be about 11 inches long. Their skin can be brown and white, or greenish yellow and brown. Like snakes, all alligator lizards shed their skin in one piece by turning it inside out as they crawl out of it. Their scales are rectangular and can expand and fold. They eat a variety of insects, including crickets, mealworms, moths, spiders, snails, and caterpillars. They can also eat small lizards, birds, and small mammals.

The granite night lizard is often found on rocky slopes with large boulders and crevices to hide in. Granite Night lizards have no eyelids; the eye is covered by a transparent spectacle or scale. They can clean their spectacles by licking them with the tongue. Granite night lizards are one of the smallest night lizards. Night lizards are active during the day, though in dark places.

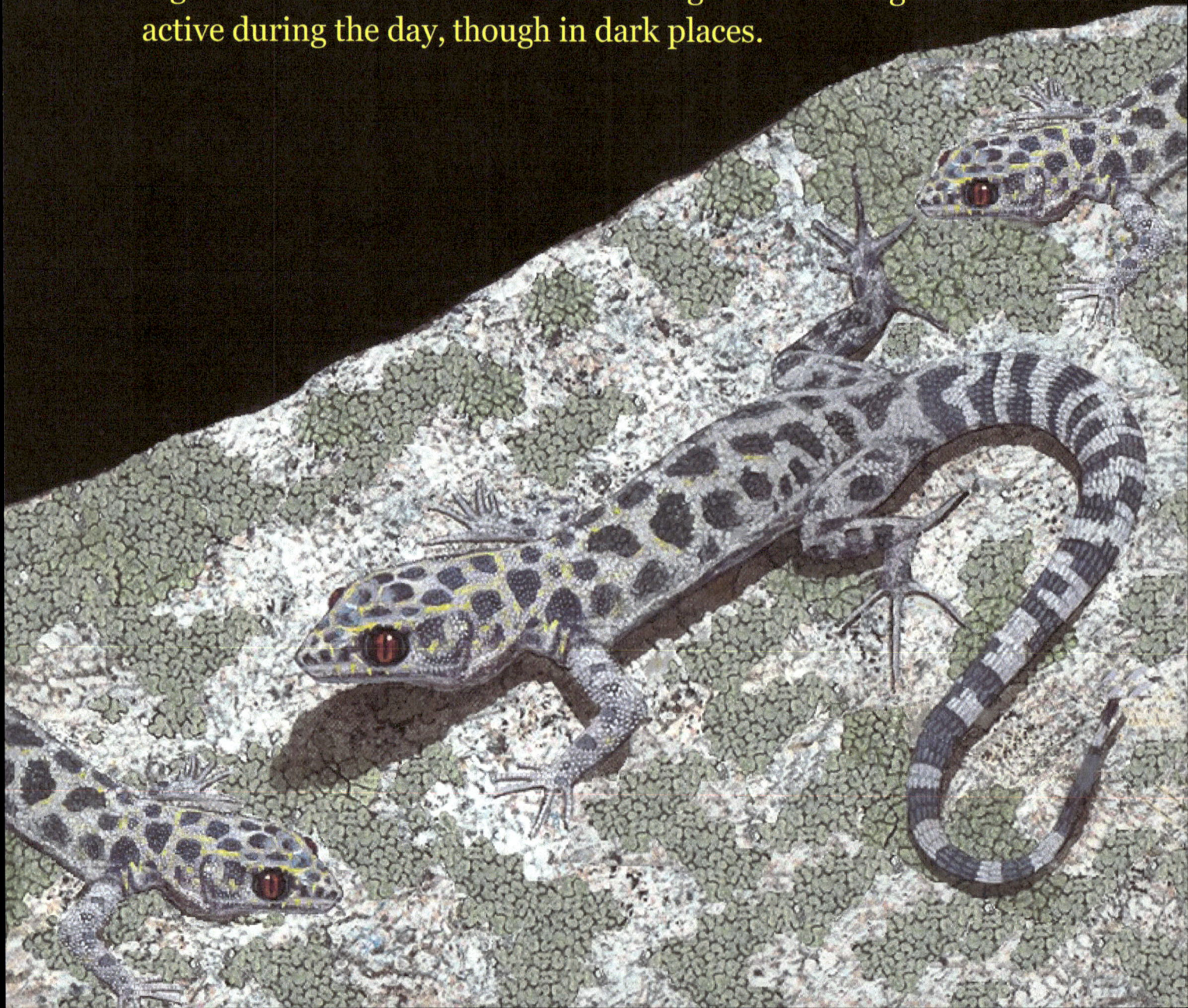

Five-lined skink lizards have five cream-colored stripes that run down their backs, their color changes with age. Males and older females, fade to a bronze color, but the stripes may still be visible. Juveniles and young adult females have a glossy black body with a blue tail. Five-lined skinks prefer humid, wooded areas with lots of cover. They are often found in bottomland forests and along wooded rivers. Five-lined skinks live in the eastern United States.

Crested Anoles can change color from light gray to reddish-brown or dark black. They change color in response to their emotions, not to camouflage themselves. Crested Anoles are very territorial and will use threat displays to establish dominance. These displays include push-ups, dewlap extensions, and head-bobbing. Crested Anoles are primarily insectivores, eating spiders, other insects, fruit, frogs, and other lizards. Crested Anoles are small lizards, growing to about 3.5 inches long. Crested Anoles perch parallel to trees, with their heads facing the ground, so they can see insects crawling on the ground.

Prairie skinks are small, brown lizards with four stripes running the length of their bodies. Juveniles are black with seven thin, yellowish stripes. Prairie skinks are excellent diggers and burrow up to 30 inches deep to escape the frost. They hibernate in their burrows from September to April. Prairie skinks can break their tails off to distract predators while escaping. The tail will grow back, but it won't be as long or colorful as the original. Prairie skinks eat small insects like crickets, grasshoppers, spiders, snails, and other arthropods.

Little brown skinks are brown, tan, or gray, with a dark brown or black stripe on each side of their back. They are woodland species that prefer to stay low to the ground and rarely climb trees. They spend most of their time hiding in the leaves. They have home ranges of less than 215 square feet. They don't travel very far. Little brown skinks use their brown color to hide in the leaves and will run away if that doesn't work. Adults are 3 to 6 inches long. Little brown skinks eat small insects, spiders, and worms.

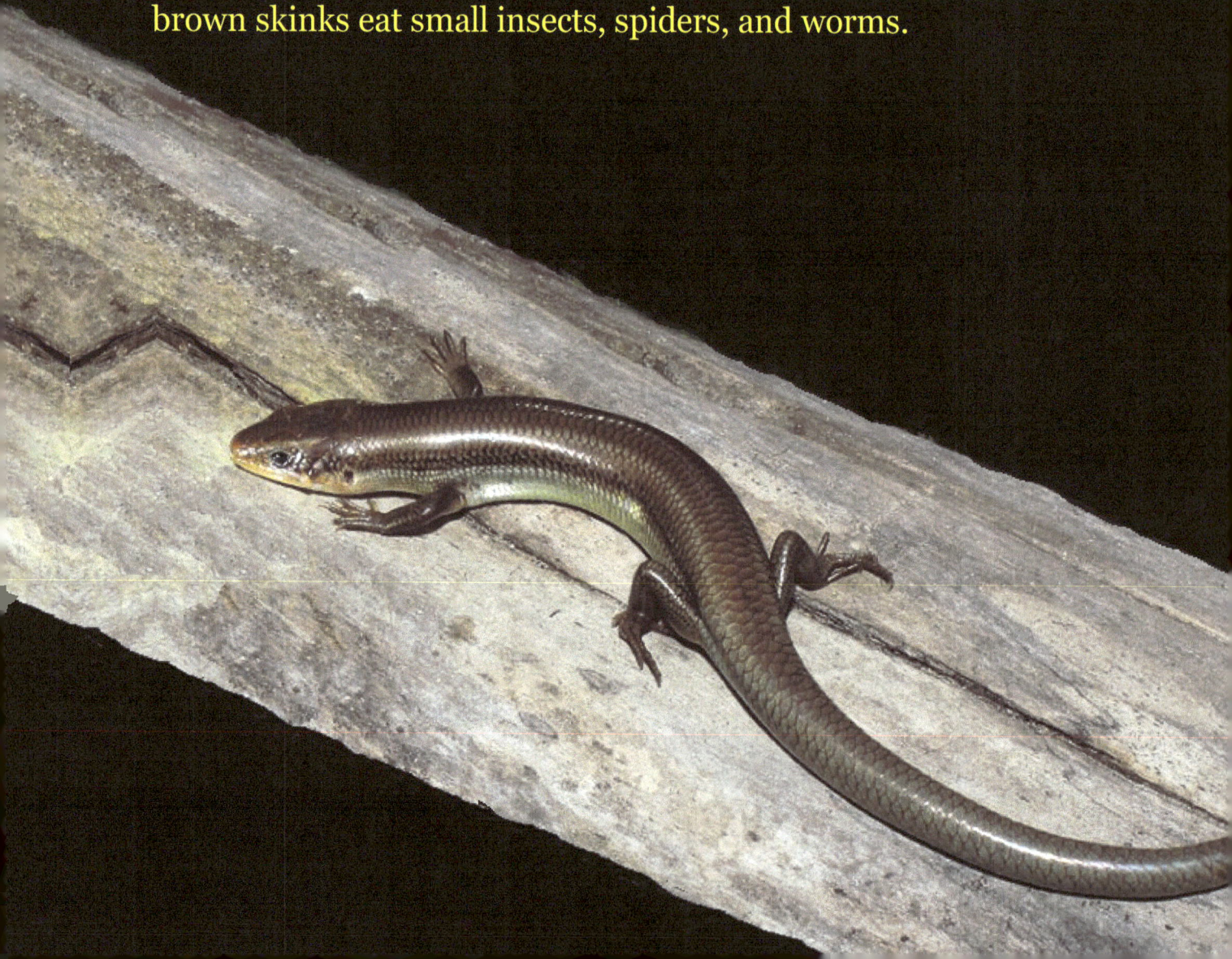

Spiny lizards have small spines on their tails and upper body. They look more like scales but are sharp. The spines help protect them from predators, if they try to grab them, they will get stung by the sharp spines. Spiny lizards also have many different colors to help them blend into their surroundings. Male spiny lizards will engage in push-up and head bobbing contests to establish dominance over their territory. Spiny lizards have a wide range of diets, they will eat almost anything. They can grow up to 13 inches long.

The name horned lizard comes from the lizard's spined back and horns on the back of its head. The spines and horns act as a defense mechanism to protect them from predators. When threatened, horned lizards can squirt blood from the ducts in the corners of their eyes to confuse predators. The blood can travel up to three feet. Horned lizards use their long sticky tongues to catch prey, rather than their jaws. Horned lizards are solitary and can be active during the day or night.

Gila monsters are named after the Gila River Basin in Arizona, where they were first discovered. The Gila monster is one of the largest lizards. Gila monsters can grow up to 22 inches long. Gila monsters have grooved teeth on their lower jaws that delivers venom when they bite. Gila monster bites are painful and can be serious, because the venom is poisonous. When they bite into their prey, the venom is injected, just like snakes, and it disables their prey, so they can eat it. Gila monsters can't jump loke other lizards. They are slow and can only run at a top speed of 1.5 miles per hour.

Garter snakes are usually recognized by their yellow stripes. Garter snakes give birth to live young, unlike most snakes that lay eggs. Garter snakes hibernate in large groups from late October to early May. Garter snakes live in a variety of habitats, including woodlands, meadows, and grassy knolls, and they like to be near water. Garter snakes can range in size from 18 to 51 inches in length. Garter snakes are poisonous, but the effects are medically insignificant and unlikely to harm humans. Garter snakes have an excellent sense of smell, which they use to detect predators and prey.

Western hognose snakes live in open prairies, meadows, and flood plains in central North America. Western hognose snakes have an upturned snout, which they use to dig in loose soil kike a hog. When threatened, western hognose snakes will flatten out their necks, inflate their bodies, and hiss. They may also strike at an intruder with their mouth closed. Western hognose snakes eat frogs, toads, salamanders, rodents, lizards, other small snakes, and eggs. Bites from western hognose snakes can cause symptoms such as pain, nausea, bleeding, and blistering.

The name kingsnake comes from the fact that they hunt and eat other snakes, which is rare for most snakes. Kingsnakes are powerful constrictors meaning that they wrap themselves around their prey and kill their prey by suffocation. Kingsnakes have bright colors and bands that flash when they move quickly, which can startle and confuse other animals. Kingsnakes eat a variety of animals, including rodents, birds, lizards, frogs, salamanders, and other snakes. Kingsnakes live in the western parts of America. Kingsnakes are among the smartest of the snake species. Their average size is between 3 to 5 feet long.

Eastern coral snakes live in the southeastern United States in wooded, sandy, and marshy areas. They eat lizards, frogs, and smaller snakes, including other coral snakes. They are venomous and are part of the elapine species. They are relatives of the cobra, mamba, and sea snake. They have two caution colors, red and yellow, which can be used as a warning to stay away. They generally only bite humans when handled or stepped on. When threatened, they may curl the tip of their tail and release gas from their cloaca to startle predators. Eastern coral snakes are typically 2 to 3 feet long but can grow to 4 feet long.

Pine snakes spend most of their time underground in burrows that they dig. They have small heads and a pointed nose and a thick neck that helps them to burrow into the ground. They hunt underground as well by raiding rodent burrows. Their color ranges from yellowish tan to white to gray or rusty brown. The Pine Snake is believed to be the rarest snake in North America. Adults can reach up to six feet in length. Pine snakes are non-venomous constrictors, but they are known to be aggressive and can deliver a powerful strike. They hiss loudly and vibrate their tails before striking.

The eastern indigo snake is the longest native snake in North America. It can grow up to 9 feet long and weigh up to 3 pounds. The eastern indigo snake is non-venomous and eats a variety of animals, including other snakes, small mammals, birds, toads, frogs, turtles, lizards, and small alligators. The eastern indigo snake is immune to the venom of other snakes and rattlesnakes. When threatened, the eastern indigo snake flattens out its neck, hisses, and vibrates its tail. The eastern indigo snake has iridescent blue-black scales and a coral-colored chin, throat, and cheeks. The eastern indigo snake likes to live in pine forest areas.

Gopher snakes are known for keeping rodent populations under control in agricultural areas. Their name is because they like to feed on rodents, like gophers. Gopher Snakes are large and heavy-bodied reptiles, reaching lengths of eight feet long. Gopher snakes live in a wide variety of habitats across North America. Gopher snakes from different habitats have different colors to help camouflage themselves with the local plants. When threatened, gopher snakes will flatten out their heads, vibrate their tails, and hiss loudly to imitate rattlesnakes. This is because they look like rattlesnakes, but they are not venomous.

Ribbon snakes are very sensitive to vibrations in the ground and have very sharp vision. They have yellow stripes against a black or dark brown body color. Ribbon snakes are good swimmers and like to live around water. They feed on tadpoles, small frogs, and small fishes. Ribbon snakes are related to Garter Snakes but are more tolerant to colder temperatures. Ribbon snakes can range in size from 16 to 41 inches long. They are not venomous. They are fast and use their speed to chase and capture prey.

Smooth green snakes also known as the grass snakes are green on top, white or pale yellow on the belly, and have a white underside on their head. Smooth green snakes live in open areas with grass and shrubs, like fields, lawns, and gardens. They can also be found in grasslands along the edges of woods. Smooth green snakes eat spiders, caterpillars, crickets, and other insects. The smooth green snake is a small to medium-sized snake that typically grows to be 14–24 inches long. Smooth green snakes are not venomous.

The Sidewinder is a rattlesnake. It got its name because it crawls in a sideways pattern. Sidewinders can move up to 18 miles per hour, making them one of the fastest snakes in the world. Sidewinders have very large fangs for a rattlesnake. The raised scales above their eyes resemble horns, it's believed that these horns may help protect the snake's eyes from the sun. Sidewinders eat rodents, lizards, and birds. Sidewinders hibernate during the winter. Sidewinder rattlesnakes can be found in sandy desert areas. Sidewinder rattlesnakes grow to 32 inches long. Sidewinders have venom, but it's weaker than other rattlesnakes. A bite can still be dangerous and require immediate medical attention.

Eastern racers color varies from cream to bright yellow. Eastern racers use their speed and agility to catch their prey. They are known to periscope, by raising their heads above the ground to get a better view of their surroundings. Eastern racers eat a variety of animals, including rodents, frogs, toads, lizards, snakes, eggs, and birds. They live in the eastern United States. They are commonly found in open habitats like grasslands, prairies, and agricultural areas. When threatened, they will coil and strike while shaking their tail nervously. They are not venomous snakes. They can grow to 6 feet long.

The copperhead is about 3 feet long. It has a pinkish or reddish body, with darker bands or blotches. Copperheads live in a variety of habitats, including forests, mixed woodlands, rock outcroppings, and low-lying, swampy regions. Copperheads have pit organs on either side of their head that help them locate objects that are warmer than their surroundings. Copperheads are venomous snakes. Their bites are painful and can cause tissue damage, but they are not fatal.

Cottonmouths get their name from the white interior of their mouths, which they expose when threatened. They are also known as water moccasins. Cottonmouths are usually brown, olive, or black with dark crossbands and light centers. Cottonmouths can grow to 48 inches long. Cottonmouths are semiaquatic, so they're comfortable both swimming in water and being on land. They are found in many areas throughout the USA. When threatened, they will vibrate their tail, throw their head back, and hiss. They may also secrete a strong odor from their anal glands. Cottonmouths are venomous and have fangs that are like tiny needles. However, they can also deliver a dry bite with no venom.

Tiger rattlesnakes got their name from their stripes. Tiger rattlesnakes have the smallest heads of any rattlesnake. Tiger rattlesnakes have one of the most toxic venoms of any rattlesnake. Their venom contains neurotoxins and mycotoxins that cause your muscles to deteriorate. Tiger rattlesnakes live in a variety of habitats, including grasslands, thorn scrub, oak forests, and hill areas. Tiger rattlesnakes are usually mild-tempered and unlikely to strike, but they will attack if agitated. Tiger rattlesnakes can grow to be 36 inches long.

Diamondback rattlesnakes got their name because they have diamond shaped patches. The Diamondback can exceed seven feet in length and is king of the desert rattlers. They are classified as pit vipers because of facial pits found below and between the eye and nostril on both sides of the head. Diamondbacks are ambush predators that use their sense of smell and infrared detection to find prey. They strike their prey with their curved fangs, injecting venom that kills red blood cells and damages tissue. Diamondbacks use their rattles to warn off predators and humans. The rattle is made of keratin, the same material as fingernails, and is a series of interlocking segments that vibrate when shaken. The snake adds a new part to its rattle each time it sheds its skin. Diamondback venom is a potent hemotoxin that can be fatal to humans.

Timber rattlesnakes got their name because they like to live in forested areas. Timber rattlesnakes are found from Canada to Texas. They are the only rattlesnake species in most of the Northern United States. They can grow to be over five feet long. Timber rattlesnakes are venomous. Their bites can cause severe facial and nerve paralysis, shock, and coagulopathy, which means your blood will not clot to plug off the wounded area. Timber rattlesnakes can recognize their siblings, even if they were separated at birth.

Alligators can't digest salt, so they live in freshwater environments like ponds, marshes, wetlands, and swamps. Male alligators can grow up to 15 feet long. Alligators Walk with their legs directly beneath them, which allows them to lift their tails off the ground. Alligators are the loudest reptiles in the world, with roars that can reach up to 90 decibels. Alligators eat a variety of foods, including bugs, amphibians, small fish, fruit, snakes, turtles, birds, and mammals. Alligators can regrow lost teeth, they have up to 80 in their mouth at one time. They can lose over 2,000 teeth in their lifetime and regrow them. They can see in the dark and their eyes glow when a light is shined on them.

Crocodiles have incredibly powerful jaws that can crush many animals. Crocodiles have 60–110 teeth, and they can replace up to 6,000 teeth in their lifetime. Their teeth are sharp. Crocodiles use their teeth to grab and hold prey. Crocodiles are fast swimmers, reaching speeds of up to 15 miles per hour. They use their strong tails to power through the water. Crocodiles can survive for months without food because they can slow down their metabolism and store fat in their bodies. Larger crocodiles can go over a year without eating. Crocodiles are reptiles, not amphibians, because they are born on land from eggs. Male crocodiles can grow to be 22 ft long and weigh over 2,200 pounds. American crocodiles can live in saltwater and are found in beaches and small islands. Crocodiles are one of the oldest living animals on the planet.

Author Page

Billy Grinslott & Kinsey Marie Books

ISBN – 9781965098516

Thanks